MXJC
5.98

PLEASE RETURN THIS ITEM
BY THE DUE DATE TO ANY
TULSA CITY-COUNTY LIBRARY.

FINES ARE 5¢ PER DAY; A
MAXIMUM OF $1.00 PER ITEM.

D0945183

United States Presidents

Thomas Jefferson

Wendie C. Old

Enslow Publishers, Inc.

44 Fadem Road   PO Box 38
Box 699   Aldershot
Springfield, NJ 07081   Hants GU12 6BP
USA   UK

Copyright © 1997 by Wendie C. Old

All rights reserved.

No part of this book may be reproduced by any means
without the written permission of the publisher.

Library of Congress Cataloging-in-Publication Data

Old, Wendie C.
    Thomas Jefferson / Wendie C. Old.
      p. cm. — (United States presidents)
    Includes bibliographical references and index.
    Summary: Explores the life of the third president, from his childhood in Virginia,
through his writing of the Declaration of Independence, to his years in office.
    ISBN 0-89490-837-5
    1. Jefferson, Thomas, 1743–1826—Juvenile literature. 2. Presidents—
United States—Biography—Juvenile literature. 3. United States—Politics and
government—1783–1809—Juvenile literature. [1. Jefferson, Thomas,
1743–1826. 2. Presidents.] I. Title. II. Series.
E332.79.O37   1997
973.4'6'092—dc21
    [B]   97-7273
                                       CIP
                                       AC

Printed in the United States of America

10 9 8 7 6 5 4 3 2 1

Illustration Credits: © 1995 Carolyn J. Yaschur, p. 95; Engraved by J. B. Forrest from a drawing by James B. Longacre after a painting by John Wesley Jarvis, Reproduced from the *Dictionary of American Portraits*, published by Dover Publications, Inc., in 1967, p. 84; Courtesy Independence National Historical Park Collection, p. 8; National Archives, pp. 11, 31, 92; Painting by Charles Willson Peale, Courtesy of Independence National Historical Park, Reproduced from the *Dictionary of American Portraits*, published by Dover Publications, Inc., in 1967, p. 64; Painting by Gilbert Stuart, Reproduced from the *Dictionary of American Portraits*, published by Dover Publications, Inc., in 1967, p. 71; Painting by Rembrandt Peale, Courtesy Princeton University, Reproduced from the *Dictionary of American Portraits*, published by Dover Publications, Inc., in 1967, p. 55; Courtesy of the Portrait Collection, Prints and Photographs Division, Library of Congress, Washington, D.C., p. 49; Prints and Photographs Division, Library of Congress, Washington, D.C., pp. 36, 40, 60, 79; Wendie C. Old, pp. 20, 21, 23, 29, 100, 103.

Source Document Credits: In David Colbert, ed., *Eyewitness to America: 500 Years of America in the Words of Those Who Saw It Happen* (New York: Pantheon Books, 1997), p. 86; Courtesy of the Colonial Williamsburg Foundation, p. 35; Facsimile from the Print Shop on Duke of Gloucester Street, Colonial Williamsburg Foundation, p. 38; In Joseph Nathan Kane, *Facts About the Presidents: A Compilation of Biographical and Historical Information* (New York: The H.W. Wilson Company, 1993), pp. 46, 80, 89; National Archives, pp. 12, 42, 52; In William A. DeGregorio, *The Complete Book of U.S. Presidents* (New York: Dembner Books, 1984), p. 65.

Cover Illustration: Thomas Jefferson, by Rembrandt Peale, 1800. White House Historical Association

j   92 J35o 1997
Old, Wendie C.
Thomas Jefferson /

Contents

TULSA CITY-COUNTY LIBRARY

1

THE COUNTRY DOUBLES IN SIZE

Thomas Jefferson became the third President of the United States of America on March 4, 1801. At that time there were fifteen states. The whole United States lay east of the Mississippi River. A large unorganized territory near the Great Lakes made up the rest of the country. It was called the Northwest Territory.

To the west was the Louisiana Territory. This area included the Mississippi River and all the land drained by it. The Territory was owned by European powers. At first it was owned and explored by the French. Later France sold it to Spain. Now there was a rumor that Spain had traded it back to France again.

Who owned this territory? The American settlers on the east bank of the Mississippi River wanted to know.

Almost half of the current American population had

built new lives there. They earned much of their money shipping goods and produce down the Mississippi River to New Orleans. This meant almost half the produce of the United States passed through a foreign city.

The goods were stored in warehouses along the river. Americans had the right to store their goods in this foreign city without paying taxes on them. This was called the Right of Deposit.

It was impossible for the settlers to send that produce over the Appalachian Mountains, even though the American cities on the Atlantic seacoast needed it. Neither wagons nor packhorses could carry as much as the river flatboats. Traveling by water was easier and faster.

Larger oceangoing ships stopped at New Orleans for the goods. They carried them up the Atlantic coast to the eastern American cities. In addition, American products were also shipped to the cities of Europe. There was an eager market overseas for American produce and goods.

What would happen if an enemy country controlled the port of New Orleans? What if the people of the United States were not allowed to sell their goods there?

For example, at this time Napoleon Bonaparte was the ruler of France. He was at the point of deciding whether to make war with England. What if France also went to war with the United States? What if the port of New Orleans was owned by France? They could close the port to American trade. This would stop the United States' Mississippi trade route. It would destroy the economy of the western half of the United States.

Jefferson discussed this with his advisors. One of Jefferson's first actions as President was to appoint a new minister to France, Robert Livingston. He asked Livingston to discover the truth about the sale. Did France or Spain own the land west of the United States? Jefferson told him to try to buy New Orleans and East and West Florida. The President also warned him not to trust Napoleon. Livingston arrived in France on December 3, 1801.

Livingston discovered that it was true. Spain had traded Louisiana to France. In exchange France gave Spain several European territories. However, Spain kept the Florida areas.

France sent a fleet to take over Hispaniola, an island in the Caribbean. (The island is now divided into Haiti and the Dominican Republic.) From this island, the French could invade the United States by way of the Louisiana Territory.

Suddenly, on October 18, 1802, the right of Americans to deposit goods in the port of New Orleans was taken away. A Spanish customs officer, Don Juan Ventura Morales, gave the order. No one knew whether he was under French or Spanish orders to do so.

American farmers arrived at the port of New Orleans in the winter of 1802–1803 as usual. However, they discovered they could not deposit their cargo in the

This portrait of Thomas Jefferson was painted from life by Charles Willson Peale. When he became President, Jefferson was very interested in expanding the territory of the United States.

warehouses. They could not sell or ship it. Their produce rotted in their flatboats or on the piers. It eventually had to be dumped into the river.

This spelled ruin for thousands of farmers. They protested to their congressmen. The congressmen demanded that President Jefferson do something about this situation.

In response, Jefferson sent his friend, James Monroe of Virginia, to France. Monroe had recently served as governor of Virginia. As a special ambassador, he was to help Livingston negotiate in France. He sailed to France on March 9.

Monroe was authorized by Jefferson to do one of two things. One was to insure Americans' rights to free passage down the Mississippi. Along with that was the right to deposit produce in New Orleans. His second option was to buy the port itself and the nearby lands.

The two negotiators were authorized by Congress to offer Napoleon from $2 million to $10 million. Napoleon Bonaparte considered the offer.

Napoleon had lost most of the troops he had sent to squash the slave rebellion on the island of Hispaniola. Some troops died from yellow fever. Others were killed in sudden night raids by rebels hidden in the hills. Napoleon would need even more troops to control the Louisiana Territory. The Louisiana property in the Americas would be just too expensive.

Napoleon needed those troops and that money if he were to declare war on Great Britain. Therefore he made a quick decision. He would get rid of his American holdings. This left him free to concentrate on the European field. He made a counteroffer.

The United States could not have New Orleans and the small patch of land around it. But, if the price were right, they could purchase all of Louisiana. What price would the United States offer him?

Being a dictator, Napoleon could make instant decisions affecting his whole country like that. However, Livingston and Monroe came from a democratic country. They were supposed to get approval from Congress for major decisions like this purchase. On the other hand, Congress was across the ocean. Traveling there and back by ship would take three or four months. Napoleon wanted their decision immediately.

Livingston and Monroe discussed this. Should they accept this offer? If they did, would Congress and the people of the United States back their decision? They examined their directions from President Jefferson. Jefferson's orders were to be flexible. They were to get the best deal possible for the United States.

The two American representatives negotiated with Napoleon and his foreign minister, Charles Talleyrand. Finally, they agreed on about $15 million for all of Louisiana.[1] The deal was struck.

Americans reacted to the news that their country had doubled in size with shock, delight, astonishment, and dismay.[2] Suddenly the United States of America was larger in size than most major powers in Europe.

Many of Jefferson's enemies accused him of loving the French. That must be why he would take their worthless real estate off their hands.

Jefferson, himself, believed the powers of the government had to be spelled out in the Constitution. Was the purchase of land a right of the President or of Congress? The Constitution said nothing. This was the first time the new country had to consider this problem. He made an executive decision to stand by the action of his ambassadors.

President Jefferson brought the completed treaty to Congress. He asked them to approve it. There was a long and bitter debate. It ended with Congress approving the treaty with Napoleon in 1803 by a huge majority. The people of the United States approved.

This map of the present United States shows how much area was added to the country by the purchase of the Louisiana Territory.

SOURCE DOCUMENT

Treaty

Between the United States of America

and the French Republic

The President of the United States of America and the First Consul of the French Republic in the name of the French People desiring to remove all Source of misunderstanding relative to objects of discussion mentioned in the Second and fifth articles of the Convention of the {8th Vendémiaire an 9 / 30 September 1800} relative to the rights claimed by the United States in virtue of the Treaty concluded at Madrid the 27 of October 1795 between His Catholic Majesty, & the Said United States, & willing to Strengthen the union and friendship which at the time of the Said Convention was happily reestablished between the two nations have respectively named their Plenipotentiaries to wit The President of the United States, by and with the advice and consent of the Senate of the Said State; Robert R. Livingston Minister Plenipotentiary of the United State, and James Monroe Minister Plenipotentiary and Envoy extraordinary of the Said State near the Government of the French Republic; And the First Consul in the name of the French people, Citizen Francis Barbé Marboire Minister of the public treasury who after having respectively exchanged their full powers have agreed to the following articles

The Louisiana Purchase Treaty of 1803.

No one knew just how much land had been purchased—not even Napoleon. The eastern border was easy to see. It was the Mississippi River. To the north it butted up against Canada. However, the southern border of Canada had yet to be drawn. The south border ran along the Gulf of Mexico until it reached Texas. The Texas area was ruled by the Spanish. Explorers later discovered that a high range of mountains (the Rocky Mountains) separated the Louisiana Purchase from the Pacific Ocean in the west.

An historian, Henry Adams, thought the purchase of the Louisiana Territory was a major achievement. It "ranked in historical importance next to the Declaration of Independence and the adoption of the Constitution."[3]

2

GROWING UP IN THE MOUNTAINS

In the seventeenth century, the Virginian colonists claimed lands all the way to the Western Sea. However, explorers discovered the continent was larger than expected. Virginia revised its claim. Now it claimed to reach west from the Atlantic Ocean to the Mississippi River. It also claimed the lands west of Pennsylvania, north to Canada.

By the 1730s, most European immigrants had settled along the eastern seaboard. Only brave and hearty souls built homes in the center of the colony.

Peter Jefferson was among them. He claimed a thousand acres along the Rivanna River. He also owned part of a nearby mountain chain. Jefferson eventually owned about seven thousand acres of rolling mountains and fertile valleys.[1]

He called his plantation along the river "Shadwell." He named it after the place in England where his wife, Jane Randolph, had been born. In the 1740s, he built a one-and-a-half-story farmhouse. When it was ready, he brought Jane and their two daughters to Shadwell.

Soon after they settled in, their son Thomas was born. His birthday was April 2, 1743 (old style calendar). Later he celebrated it on April 13 (new style calendar). This confusing set of double dates was caused by a change in calendars.

When Thomas Jefferson was born, Great Britain and its colonies were still using the Julian calendar. This old calendar was created by the Roman emperor, Julius Caesar, in 46 B.C. By the 1700s this calendar no longer matched the seasons of the year. The more accurate Gregorian calendar corrects the error.

In 1750, the British Parliament adopted the Gregorian calendar. This action shifted many dates by eleven days. Thus Thomas Jefferson's birthday shifted to April 13.

When Thomas was about three years old, Peter Jefferson's best friend, William Randolph, died. His will asked Peter Jefferson and his family to live on Randolph's plantation. It was called Tuckahoe. This way, Jefferson could care for Randolph's three orphaned children.

Thomas remembered moving from Shadwell to Tuckahoe. It was one of his earliest memories. He rode there on a horse while one of his father's slaves sat behind him and held him firmly. Thomas sat on a pillow balanced on the saddle. This cushioned the jolting fifty-mile ride.

The area around Tuckahoe was not as lonely as Shadwell for Thomas's mother. It was closer to other eastern British settlements. It sat near the banks of the upper James River. The house was large enough for both families. It was two stories high and built in the shape of an "H." The Randolph family lived in one wing. The Jeffersons lived in the other. The families shared the central common rooms.

They lived there for six years. More children were born. Thomas already had two older sisters. Soon he had four younger sisters and a younger brother. They all grew up alongside the Randolph children. To escape the crowd of noisy, active children, Thomas read books or explored nature.

He enjoyed hiking through the woods on the nearby hillsides.[2] He searched for deer, turkey, and other wild game. He rode horses. He learned to paddle a canoe. He learned to hunt and to shoot. He kept his love of learning through books and learning about nature throughout his life.

His mother's family, the Randolphs, were Virginia aristocrats. His father, on the other hand, was a self-taught man. Peter Jefferson loved learning for learning's sake. He passed that desire for knowledge to his children.

Thomas's father taught himself to survey land.

Surveyors measure land, marking the borders of people's properties. Their findings are then recorded. People needed surveyors in western Virginia. This helped everyone know just how much land they owned.

Peter Jefferson became assistant county surveyor. He helped Joshua Fry, the county surveyor. They surveyed the southern boundary of the colony of Virginia. Together they created an accurate map of Virginia. The map was published in 1751.

Thomas's father entertained his children with tales about his surveying trips. One time they had to eat raw deer and bear meat because it was too wet to make a fire. Another time they slept in trees to escape wildcats and wolves.

Throughout his life, Peter Jefferson held many public offices. He had been sheriff and also a judge. Eventually he represented his county in the House of Burgesses. This group of men helped govern the colony of Virginia. It met in Williamsburg, the capital of Virginia.

Tuckahoe Plantation swarmed with children. A small school was set up to educate them. Thomas learned to read, write, and keep farm accounts. He did not do well when asked to speak up in class. His tongue did not seem to be able to keep up with his thoughts. He did better when he wrote down his words.

Thomas found many strange ideas about America in his textbooks. These books had not been written by people who lived in America. They had been written overseas in Great Britain.

One claimed the American wildlife was smaller and weaker than European wildlife. Another said the weather in America was unhealthy. A third said American children would grow up shorter than European children. Thomas's father assured him that the books were wrong.

Thomas went with his father on some surveying trips. He learned how to survey. The two of them identified different rocks and trees they found.

Peter Jefferson taught Thomas the many skills necessary to run a large plantation. He told Thomas, "Never . . . ask another to do for you what you can do for yourself."[3]

Eventually Peter Jefferson took his family back to Shadwell. However, Thomas did not go with them. At age nine, he went to live with a Scottish clergyman named William Douglas. He continued his education at the school in Douglas's house. Thomas spent five years there. He visited Shadwell during vacations.

During those vacations, he explored the lands his father owned. He climbed a nearby mountaintop at least once during each visit. It was not the tallest peak the Jeffersons owned, but it was a special place for Thomas.

His father was a warmhearted man whose house was always open to his friends and neighbors. Even the nearby Native Americans thought of him as a friend.

They would stop and visit on their trips to the capital of Virginia. Thomas inherited his father's generosity and kindness.

Peter Jefferson died when Thomas was fourteen years old. As the oldest son, he was the head of the family. In his will, Peter Jefferson left all his books (forty of them) to Thomas. He also insisted that his son get a classical education. This meant that Thomas should continue his studies and go to college.

Thomas moved to a school closer to Shadwell. It was run by the Reverend James Maury. He could come home on weekends. During these two years he took Greek, Latin, and French, plus dancing lessons. In addition, he learned to play the violin. He continued to play it throughout his life.

He lived at the reverend's home, along with other students. He was allowed to spend his spare time reading from the four hundred books in Maury's library. This sparked Jefferson's lifelong love of books.

College for Thomas meant the College of William and Mary in Williamsburg, Virginia. He left for school in December 1759. He was nearly full grown. Although well-mannered and well-liked, with a charmingly low voice, he was not actually handsome. He was lean, bony, and broad shouldered with a thin neck and red hair. His face tended to blush a lot. His height, over six feet, inspired nicknames like "Long Tom."

Williamsburg at that time was the political, social, and cultural center of the upper South. The college

This is the Wren Building at the College of William and Mary in Williamsburg, where Jefferson lived and took classes. The college faced the House of Burgesses at the other end of the one-mile main street of colonial Williamsburg.

stood at one end of the Duke of Gloucester Street. The House of Burgesses faced it at the other end. The Governor's Palace on one side made the third point of the political triangle. There were seventy-five students at the college (eight were Native Americans). They found themselves caught up in the social, intellectual, and political events in the town.

Jefferson registered as a student of philosophy in March 1760. In the 1700s, philosophy schools taught what we would now call science.

He found himself with the only teacher who was not

a reverend of the Church of England. Dr. William Small introduced Jefferson to the exciting world of ideas. He also pulled Jefferson into his circle of friends. These were professor of law George Wythe and the acting governor of Virginia, Francis Fauquier. Fauquier was considered to be the most capable man to fill that office.

They often dined together in the Governor's Palace. These were evenings of fine food, good company, and conversation that struck fire. Jefferson added his violin to the musical evenings when everyone played an instrument.

At school, everything interested him. He studied Spanish, Greek, Latin, French, Anglo-Saxon, Newtonian

This is the House of Burgesses in Williamsburg. The men appointed to be in the Royal Governor's council met on the left. The Virginia House of Burgesses met on the right. The two groups met together in the room over the archways to settle differences.

physics, mathematics, science, philosophy, rhetoric, and literature.

He was introduced to the beliefs of the Enlightenment movement. One of them is the idea that mankind is in control of its own destiny. Jefferson joined the people of the Age of Reason.

He sometimes studied fifteen hours a day. However, he remembered his father's instructions to keep his body as strong as his mind. He often took a break to run a mile outside of Williamsburg and back. As most college students do, he flirted with girls and joined secret clubs.

When he was nineteen, he fell in love with sixteen-year-old Rebecca Burwell. He called her Belinda. He wrote awkward, romantic poetry to her. However, he never sent it. He moped around. He told his friends how much he loved her. However, he was unable to complete a full sentence in her presence. For several years he loved her from afar.

He finally gathered enough courage to tell her, in his timid way, about his feelings. However, she was already interested in another man and married him soon after. Jefferson tried to forget her. He decided he would never get married. He went back to studying even harder.

In 1762, he left the college to study law with George Wythe. He hated law, and made fun of it and all its strange jargon.[4] He was required to read about British rights and liberties. This laid a firm foundation for his future political beliefs.

In addition to studying law, he was able to watch the way the government of Virginia worked in the nearby House of Burgesses. He joined the crowd in the doorway on May 30, 1765. His friend, Patrick Henry, spoke in support of the Stamp Act Resolutions. The Resolutions opposed the Stamp Act—the British law that demanded that the American colonies must pay for and place a stamp on their legal documents. The more conservative members of the House shouted "Treason!" This did not stop Henry. He continued, "If this be treason, make the most of it."[5]

The speech inspired the Virginia House of Burgesses. They resolved that Parliament did not have the right to

George Wythe's law office and study in Williamsburg, Virginia. Thomas Jefferson studied law with Wythe here for five years.

impose tax laws on the colonies. Jefferson saw how one man's words can influence a group.

While he studied law, Jefferson turned twenty-one. He could then legally take an active part in managing his inherited land. He chose the Rivanna lands (including the grist mill and his favorite mountaintop). Jefferson also inherited twenty-two of his father's slaves. His younger brother inherited an equally large piece of land on the Fluvanna River. Jefferson's sisters also inherited part of their father's estate.

Jefferson spent part of the next few years at Shadwell. He brought along his assigned readings and continued his law studies in the evenings. Jefferson worked at his law studies both at Shadwell and at Williamsburg for five years. In 1767 he passed all the tests necessary for becoming a lawyer. He was ready to take his place in the Virginia colony's government.

3

BEGINNINGS— MONTICELLO AND POLITICAL LIFE

Before Jefferson could work in government, he needed a home base. He built a thriving law practice in Albemarle County. He hired workers to flatten off the rounded top of his favorite mountain.

This was not the highest peak in the mountain chain. It was only 987 feet high. The sides sloped gently. They supported fruit orchards. Jefferson chose the sunny southern side for his vegetable garden. He had men flatten out a large area near the top of the mountain for it. He later wrote, "No occupation is so delightful to me as the culture of . . . the garden."[1]

He kept detailed notes in a journal. Every morning of his life, he wrote in his *Garden Book*. In it he noted every seed, tree, and bush planted. Using a carefully trimmed goose-quill pen, he even kept records of every day's weather.

Jefferson called his mountaintop plantation Monticello. The name is Italian for "little mountain." He spent the next fifty years planning, building, and redesigning the house and grounds. He wrote, "Architecture is my delight, and putting up, and pulling down, one of my favorite amusements."[2] From this mountaintop perch he had marvelous views of the countryside. He could see all the way to the Blue Ridge Mountains in the west.

Jefferson studied books about architecture. He made sketches for the main house at Monticello. They were based on the style of a sixteenth-century Italian architect, Andrea Palladio. Palladio built villas whose designs were based on still older Roman buildings.

Jefferson's plan called for a large central house. A wooden walkway jutted out from each side of the house. Under one walkway were the stables. The other walkway covered the kitchen. Some house slaves also lived there. The walkways ended at two small outbuildings.

The first buildings on the mountaintop were wooden houses for the slaves and other workers. Next came sheds to protect the work areas from the weather. A kiln was built to make bricks. Most houses in that area of Virginia were built of wood. However, Jefferson insisted on brick. This would have a clean, classical look and would be more permanent than wood.

Next, a one-room brick outbuilding was built. Jefferson immediately moved into it to oversee the work. He ordered V-shaped troughs built under the wooden walkways. The troughs collected rainwater dripping through the slats of the walkway. More V-shaped troughs were placed on the roof of the main house.

All these water collectors filled the water cisterns. Lots of water was needed every day for the large number of people living at Monticello. The shallow, hand-dug well did not supply enough. The cisterns provided more water.

Monticello was built slowly. Meanwhile, Jefferson followed his father's footsteps into political office. He inherited his father's position as justice of the peace. In December 1768, he was elected to the Virginia House of Burgesses. He was one of the two delegates from Albemarle County.

This was to be the shortest session in the history of Virginia. Jefferson took his seat in the House on May 8, 1769. His mother's cousin, Peyton Randolph, was elected speaker of the House. Because of this family connection, Jefferson was put on two important committees.

All colonial governors at that time were appointed by the king of Great Britain. The fifty-year-old Right Honorable Norborne Berkley, Baron de Botetourt, formally opened the first meeting of the House with a speech.

Jefferson's first attempt at political writing was to

draft a response to this speech. Unfortunately, his words were thrown out by the committee. They rewrote it. This crushed the young representative. He spent the rest of the ten-day session quietly watching.

On the ninth day the House of Burgesses passed several resolutions. One of the resolutions insisted that they had the sole right to levy taxes in the colony, not the British Parliament. Immediately, the governor, a British official, dissolved the House of Burgesses.

Later, most of the House of Burgesses met in the center of Williamsburg at Raleigh Tavern. This informal group included George Washington. He brought more resolutions before the group to sign. This was the first important public paper Jefferson ever signed.

The governor allowed new elections in August. All the men who met at the tavern were reelected. Those who had avoided the meeting were not. Jefferson continued to be reelected to the House of Burgesses for the next few years.

In 1770 the house at Shadwell burned to the ground. The family escaped. Unfortunately, most of the library and all the letters and papers about Jefferson's law cases were destroyed. Luckily for Jefferson, his violin and a few precious books were rescued. Twenty more books were miles away, safe in his Williamsburg law office.

Jefferson's mother and brothers and sisters moved up onto the mountaintop. They moved into the

This is the Raleigh Tavern in Williamsburg, Virginia. The House of Burgesses would meet here when the royal governor officially disbanded them.

overseer's house. The first section of the main house was not completed until 1775.

Neither the Shadwell plantation nor Monticello made much profit. Slavery was beginning to cost too much. Feeding and clothing the slaves ate up whatever profits they produced. Tobacco sales brought in less and less income. The Shadwell sawmill and Jefferson's law practice supported the family living on the mountaintop.

Naturally Jefferson took part in the political and social life in Williamsburg. He met a lively widow—Martha Wayles Skelton—daughter of another lawyer, John Wayles. He visited often at their home, called The Forest. It sat by the nearby James River. Martha had lovely brown hair with auburn highlights and flashing hazel eyes. She also had a sense of humor and a love of books and music.

The two of them were constantly together. Jefferson and Martha played duets on violin and harpsichord. Jefferson courted the wealthy, warm-hearted widow for two years.

The couple married at Martha's father's house on New Year's Day, 1772. Two weeks later they set out for Monticello. In Albemarle County they hit one of the worst snowstorms of the decade. The snow piled several feet deep. They had to leave the carriage near Charlottesville. The couple rode horseback eight miles along twisty mountain roads to Monticello.

They arrived long after dark. The servants had given up expecting them and had gone to bed. Jefferson did not disturb them. He stabled the horses himself. Then the two newlyweds settled in the one-room brick house near the partly completed big house.

The cheerful, loving, sweet-tempered Martha knew how to run a plantation. The happy young couple were deeply in love.[3] On September 27, 1772, their first child, Martha, was born.

On May 28, 1773, Jefferson's father-in-law died. The land the couple inherited put them in the class of the greatest landholders in Virginia. The Jeffersons also loved to entertain and live well. Selling some of that land helped them buy luxuries. Later it helped buy furnishings for Monticello.

This inheritance also allowed Jefferson to stop

practicing law. He now concentrated on running the plantations he owned. He also had more time for his political life.

In addition, he became active in the underground Virginia Committee of Correspondence. Similar committees linked people in most of the American colonies. They insured that events in one colony would quickly be known in others. As a result, soon the colonies were making plans to meet and work together.

To the north of Virginia, in Boston, Massachusetts, some people protested the tax on tea. On December 16, 1773, they dressed as Native Americans and dumped a load of tea into the harbor. The British immediately closed Boston Harbor to trade. This ruined the business

This etching shows the Boston Tea Party, which inspired the other American colonies to support the protests of Massachusetts against British authority.

of Boston merchants who depended upon goods arriving by sea. The other colonies heard and quickly responded.

The Virginia House of Burgesses drafted a resolution supporting the Bostonians. This action appalled the newly appointed Governor Dunmore. (His full name was His Excellency John Murray, Earl of Dunmore, Viscount Fincastle, Baron of Blair, of Moulin, and of Tillymont.) The governor immediately dissolved the body of lawmakers. Again the Burgesses simply moved to the Raleigh Tavern and reassembled.

At this point the Burgesses voted to boycott British imports. They also sent letters to the other colonies. The letters urged a meeting of representatives of all the British colonies.

Jefferson returned to Monticello. He put his thoughts together into a pamphlet. It was published in the summer of 1774 as *A Summary View of the Rights of British America*. The lanky, freckled, sandy-haired Jefferson became recognized as a forceful political writer.

4

THE DECLARATION OF INDEPENDENCE

The First Continental Congress gathered in Philadelphia in 1774. This was the first time representatives of all the English-speaking American colonies met together. Here they could discuss mutual problems.

Thomas Jefferson was among those chosen to represent Virginia. However, he was not able to attend because he became sick. He sent his pamphlet to be passed among the delegates.

Early in 1775, the Virginia House of Burgesses delegates met at Richmond, Virginia. They discussed the decisions of the First Continental Congress. This was the first meeting of the Burgesses away from the governor in Williamsburg. Jefferson attended.

At this meeting Patrick Henry pushed for action. He

proclaimed, "Give me liberty, or give me death."[1] Jefferson also made a speech. However, his writing skills were more appreciated. He drafted the Virginia Plan for a militia to defend the colony.

The Second Continental Congress met on May 10, 1775. Jefferson became one of the Virginia delegates. The American Revolution had begun. The battles of Lexington and Concord had been fought in April. The American Army surrounded Boston.

Before Jefferson could leave for Philadelphia, Governor Dunmore called a session of the House of Burgesses at Williamsburg. They were to discuss important news from overseas. Great Britain's new Prime Minister, Lord Frederick North, had tried to stop the rebellion in the colonies with a peace offer.

Jefferson stayed a few days to help draft Virginia's response. This was called the Virginia Resolutions. The discussion grew so violent that Governor Dunmore moved out of Williamsburg. He fled aboard a British ship docked nearby. Dunmore tried to continue ruling Virginia from shipboard throughout the American Revolution. The ship sailed around the Chesapeake Bay and up Virginia's rivers. Eventually, most Virginians ignored him.

The Virginia Resolutions refused the peace offer. They insisted that the House of Burgesses was a ruling body equal to Parliament. Parliament ruled only in Great Britain. It had no right to involve itself in the

SOURCE DOCUMENT

A

SUMMARY VIEW

OF THE

RIGHTS

OF

BRITISH AMERICA.

SET FORTH IN SOME

RESOLUTIONS

INTENDED FOR THE

INSPECTION

OF THE PRESENT

DELEGATES

OF THE

PEOPLE OF VIRGINIA.

NOW IN

CONVENTION.

BY A NATIVE, AND MEMBER OF THE
HOUSE OF BURGESSES.

WILLIAMSBURG:
PRINTED BY CLEMENTINA RIND

This pamphlet was written by Thomas Jefferson in 1774. It was passed among the members of the First Continental Congress. As a result, Jefferson became known as a fine writer.

colonies' private affairs. Only the Burgesses could do that.

Resolutions in hand, Jefferson arrived in Philadelphia on June 21, 1775. He discovered he already knew most of the men at the Continental Congress. In return, they knew of him and his writings.

Fellow Virginian, George Washington, had been named commander in chief of the continental forces. He left to take command in Boston soon after Jefferson arrived.

John Adams described Jefferson as being shy in public but charming in private parties and committee

This is Independence Hall in Philadelphia, Pennsylvania. The city was the central point in the thirteen colonies, which made it a good place for the Continental Congress to meet.

work. He was aware of Jefferson's "reputation for literature, science, and a happy talent of composition."[2] The congress nominated Jefferson to be on the committee to draw up a declaration of war. This "Declaration of the Causes and Necessity of taking up Arms" was published and widely read. Jefferson returned home in August 1775.

Governor Dunmore issued proclamations and orders from shipboard throughout the fall. In January 1776, he ordered his ship and others to fire upon the city of Norfolk, Virginia. This did not bring the colony back under his control. It only helped drive the Virginia colony to outright revolt.

Also in January 1776, a pamphlet called *Common Sense* by Thomas Paine sparked more rebellion. The forty-seven-page pamphlet was not full of common sense. It was an attack on the right of kings to rule free people. Paine urged Americans to break away from Great Britain and establish a nation of freedom. Sales rose to over five hundred thousand copies. Even George Washington praised it.

By May 13, 1776, Jefferson was back at the Second Continental Congress. On Friday, June 7, 1776, Richard Henry Lee introduced a resolution that the connection between the United Colonies and the state of Great Britain should be broken. This shocking idea was debated through the next Tuesday. Then debate was postponed until July 1.

A paper was necessary to explain to the world just

SOURCE DOCUMENT

By His Excellency the Right Honorable JOHN Earl of DUNMORE, His MAJESTY's Lieutenant and Governor General of the Colony and Dominion of VIRGINIA, and Vice Admiral of the same.

A PROCLAMATION.

AS I have ever entertained Hopes that an Accomodation might have taken Place between GREAT-BRITAIN and this Colony, without being compelled by my Duty to this moſt diſagreeable but now abſolutely neceſſary Step, rendered ſo by a Body of armed Men unlawfully aſſembled, firing on His MAJESTY's Tenders, and the formation of an Army, and that Army now on their March to attack His MAJESTY's Troops and deſtroy the well diſpoſed Subjects of this Colony. To defeat ſuch treaſonable Purpoſes, and that all ſuch Traitors, and their Abettors, may be brought to Juſtice, and that the Peace, and good Order of this Colony may be again reſtored, which the ordinary Courſe of the Civil Law is unable to effect ; I have thought fit to iſſue this my Proclamation, hereby declaring, that until the aforeſaid good Purpoſes can be obtained, I do in Virtue of the Power and Authority to ME given, by His MAJESTY, determine to execute Martial Law, and cauſe the ſame to be executed throughout this Colony: and to the end that Peace and good Order may the ſooner be reſtored, I do require every Perſon capable of bearing Arms, to reſort to His MAJESTY's STANDARD, or be looked upon as Traitors to His MAJESTY's Crown and Government, and thereby become liable to the Penalty the Law inflicts upon ſuch Offences; ſuch as forfeiture of Life, confiſcation of Lands, &c. &c. And I do hereby further declare all indentured Servants, Negroes or others, (appertaining to Rebels,) free that are able and willing to bear Arms, they joining His MAJESTY's Troops as ſoon as may be, for the more ſpeedily reducing this Colony to a proper Senſe of their Duty, to His MAJESTY's Crown and Dignity. I do further order, and require, all His MAJESTY's Leige Subjects, to retain their Quitrents, or any other Taxes due or that may become due, in their own Cuſtody, till ſuch Time as Peace may be again reſtored to this at preſent moſt unhappy Country, or demanded of them for their former ſalutary Purpoſes, by Officers properly authoriſed to receive the ſame.

GIVEN under my Hand on board the Ship WILLIAM, off NORFOLK, the 7th Day of NOVEMBER, in the SIXTEENTH Year of His MAJESTY's Reign.

DUNMORE.

(GOD ſave the KING.)

This is one of the many useless proclamations issued by Governor Dunmore during the American Revolution while he was safe in a British ship in the Chesapeake. The people of Virginia ignored him.

why the American colonies were separating from Great Britain—a Declaration of Independence. Congress appointed a committee of five men to prepare it. Thomas Jefferson was one of the youngest men there. However, he was a natural choice.

He was thirty-three years old and an educated gentleman. Jefferson could "calculate an eclipse, survey an estate, tie an artery, plan an edifice [house], try a cause, break a horse, dance a minuet and play the violin."[3] Everyone knew he was not a good public speaker. However, his writing skills were the best.

The other four men were also good writers. John Adams of Massachusetts, Benjamin Franklin of Pennsylvania, Roger Sherman of Connecticut, and Robert R. Livingston of New York made up the committee. The four represented the southern, central, and northern colonies.

The committee members unanimously decided Jefferson should write the first draft. Jefferson struggled to put the words down on paper for seventeen days. He used his new portable writing desk.

At the same time he wrote a constitution for the newly independent state of Virginia. His version reached Virginia too late, however. The committee working on the state constitution had already adopted one written by George Mason. They used Jefferson's suggestions to improve Mason's draft.

Jefferson discussed his draft of the Declaration with

The committee in charge of writing the Declaration of Independence included (from left to right): Thomas Jefferson (Virginia), John Adams (Massachusetts), Benjamin Franklin (Pennsylvania), Roger Sherman (Connecticut), and Robert Livingston (New York).

the rest of the committee. They made a few changes. On June 28, Jefferson's words were presented to Congress.

Most of the representatives there were lawyers. They set out to improve the Declaration. Their suggestions removed about one fourth of the words and altered others. Jefferson suffered silently as his words were torn apart. He winced when the arguments about his words grew hot.[4] John Adams was a better debater than Jefferson. Adams fought for every phrase. At times it took an hour for the group to agree on a single word. By July 3, most of the representatives agreed with the revision.

Congress then took up Richard Henry Lee's resolution for independence. On July 4, they agreed to add it to the last paragraph of the Declaration of Independence.

The first sentences of the Declaration display genuine American attitudes. They discuss the natural rights of people, government by the agreement of the governed, and the natural right of revolution against bad government. These opening words were among the few not changed by the Congress. They are, in fact, Jefferson's own words:

> When in the course of human events, it becomes necessary for one people to dissolve the political bonds which have connected them with another, and to assume among the powers of the earth, the separate and equal station to which the laws of nature and of nature's God entitle them, a decent respect to the opinions of mankind requires that they should declare the causes which impel them to the separation.
>
> We hold these truths to be self-evident, that all men are created equal, that they are endowed by their Creator with certain unalienable rights; that among these are life, liberty, and the pursuit of happiness.[5]

Jefferson explained later that his main purpose was

> not to find . . . new arguments . . . but . . . the common sense of the subject, in terms so plain and firm as to command . . . [agreement], and to justify ourselves in the independent stand we [must] take . . . and to give that expression the proper tone and spirit called for by the occasion.[6]

Jefferson owned slaves. No large plantation could be run without them in those days. How could a

SOURCE DOCUMENT

This is a reproduction of the Declaration of Independence, written by Thomas Jefferson in 1776.

slaveholder believe that "all men are created equal?" Jefferson had studied the philosophers of the Age of Reason and the Enlightenment. He agreed that slavery was against the law of nature. Wicked human laws had created slavery. Jefferson expected that such laws would be repealed over time.[7]

He had included a paragraph attacking slavery in his first draft. However, the Congress knew that representatives of certain colonies would not sign if it had an antislavery clause. Therefore, they removed it.

All members of the Second Continental Congress signed the Declaration of Independence. Congress ordered it printed without the signatures. Copies of this printing were sent to every unit in the army. It was also sent to every town in the country. It was read to all the people.

Members of Congress took a great risk in signing this document. They realized they were, as the last sentence of the Declaration said, trusting each other with "our Lives, our Fortunes, and our sacred Honor."[8]

By this act, they now were traitors. They were enemies of the British. Signers could be hanged if caught. During the war, many of the signers had their homes looted and their businesses or farms destroyed. Some were put in prison.

5

WAR AND PEACE

Jefferson resigned from Congress in September 1776. His wife was not well. After each of their children was born, she became sick. Jefferson did not know what was happening at Monticello. Mail could take several weeks to get from there to Philadelphia.

All summer long, Congress had been creating the plan of Confederation. This would knit the colonies together into one country. However, Jefferson felt the main powers of government would be held by the states, not by a national government. He wanted to take part in creating the new state of Virginia.[1]

He visited Monticello. In October 1776, he took his seat in the Virginia House of Delegates. His wife and children came with him to Williamsburg. On August 1, 1778, another daughter, named Mary was born.

He wanted the American Revolution to be more than a break from Great Britain. He intended to help change both the law of the land and the social order. Jefferson spent the next few years in various Virginia House of Delegate committees revising the law.

Several of Jefferson's bills slowed down the power of the aristocracy in Virginia. They lay a base for a truly republican government by the people and for the people. Normally only the oldest child inherited the land and wealth. This left the rest of the children poor. One of his bills stopped this. From then on the power and wealth of the aristocracy became divided.

Other bills laid the foundation for an enlightened state full of educated free men. One established a public library. Others supplied free education. It would be free for the most talented of all classes of people—rich and poor.

Jefferson was most proud of one bill. It was the Bill for Establishing Religious Freedom, passed in 1779.[2] Before this bill, all citizens in the colonies had to pay a tax to support the official religion. The official religion was the Church of England. All other beliefs were considered unofficial. The tax supported the upkeep of the official church buildings. It also paid the salaries of the clergy of the official state church.

Jefferson's bill was a new idea at the time. Nowhere else were people free to worship any way they pleased. Most countries had an official religion. This idea of religious freedom was eventually copied by the rest of the United States.

Time and time again, Jefferson condemned slavery. He saw it as an evil that must be eliminated. None of his proposals to change slavery laws were ever able to get out of committee to become bills. His views were mild by modern standards, but they were too advanced for his time.

One of his proposals was to free every slave born after a certain date. The free slaves would be deported. He could not see freed slaves and their old masters ever living in peaceful equality. Jefferson was a product of his times. He could not see them as equals.

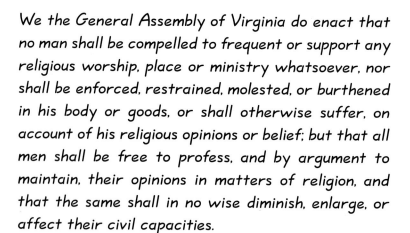

SOURCE DOCUMENT

We the General Assembly of Virginia do enact that no man shall be compelled to frequent or support any religious worship, place or ministry whatsoever, nor shall be enforced, restrained, molested, or burthened in his body or goods, or shall otherwise suffer, on account of his religious opinions or belief; but that all men shall be free to profess, and by argument to maintain, their opinions in matters of religion, and that the same shall in no wise diminish, enlarge, or affect their civil capacities.

This is an excerpt from Jefferson's bill establishing religious freedom in Virginia, which was enacted by the Virginia Legislature in 1779.

His political activity led to people electing him governor of Virginia on June 1, 1779. He followed his friend, Patrick Henry. Henry had been governor of Virginia for three years. James Monroe became Jefferson's aide. They stayed friends for the rest of their lives.

Meanwhile, the American Revolution ground on. Most of the early battles were in the northern states. The Carolinas and Georgia in the South were invaded in 1780. Virginia expected fighting along its coast any minute.

Jefferson sent supplies to the northern and southern battlefronts. He sent food, equipment, and soldiers. The amount he sent was never enough. However, sending all those supplies left Virginia quite defenseless.

In 1781, near the end of Jefferson's second term, General Lord Charles Cornwallis invaded Virginia. He attacked the new capital, Richmond. The government body fled to Charlottesville. British soldiers pursued them. They especially wanted to capture Jefferson. By this time everyone, including the British, knew he had written the Declaration of Independence.

Captain Jack Jouett spied the British advancing. He raced five and a half hours through the night. He followed hidden mountain paths to warn the legislature. They moved west over the Blue Ridge Mountains to the Shenandoah Valley. The British, following close behind, captured a few of them.

Jefferson was not with them. His term as governor

had ended on June 1, 1781. He rode his horse up to Monticello. The British arrived in Charlottesville on June 4. They advanced up his little mountain hoping to capture him.

Jefferson helped Martha and their four children pack. Martha was ill. She had not yet recovered from the birth of their daughter Mary in 1778. Jefferson sent his family to Poplar Forest, one of their other plantations.

Jefferson stayed behind. He worked at destroying and hiding his papers until almost the last minute. Then he fled through the woods. For a time people considered him a coward for running away.

What one man could have done against an army, Jefferson did not know. He stood in the legislature the next year to face his accusers. The House of Delegates declared the charges groundless. In addition, they voted to award him thanks. However, Jefferson was humiliated by the accusation. He bitterly declared he would never run for office again.[3]

He was back home at Monticello when Cornwallis surrendered at the battle of Yorktown, Virginia, in October 1781. It would be several more years before the official peace treaty was signed.

The Jeffersons had one son and five daughters. However, only two reached adulthood. These two were Martha, who was named for her mother, and Mary.

Each time Martha Jefferson had a child, her health grew worse. Their last child, Lucy, was born in May

This silhouette is the only known portrait of Thomas Jefferson's beloved wife, Martha.

1782. Martha never recovered from the birth. She died on September 6, 1782. Thomas Jefferson collapsed in sorrow. He had lost the cherished companion of his life. He swore on her deathbed that he would never remarry. He never did.

He shut himself into his room for three weeks. Finally, his daughter Martha convinced him to come out. He was needed to make decisions about running Monticello and his other plantations. They spent hours riding on horseback through the countryside, shedding tears of grief.

Jefferson worked on new designs for the architecture of Monticello. He made scientific observations. Jefferson also created new inventions. He even bought other people's inventions if they seemed useful.

He had a dumbwaiter built along the side of the fireplace mantelpiece in the dining room. It was just large enough to carry up one bottle of wine. The other box alongside it held an empty bottle. The boxes traveled from the dining room to a passageway under the house.

Built into the dining room door was another clever Jefferson idea. Three half-circle shelves were attached to a door panel. The kitchen slaves would place the hot food on them. When the family and guests were ready to eat, the panel was turned into the dining room. The dining room servants then served the food. Sometimes the family would help themselves. Dirty dishes were piled on the shelves for the slaves to remove later.

Jefferson could not stay away from the political

scene for long. He was elected again to the Confederation Congress in 1783. Philadelphia was still in British hands. The temporary capital of the country had been moved to Annapolis, Maryland.

That year the Treaty of Paris was signed. This officially ended the American Revolution. Gradually, British troops left the country.

Jefferson worked to organize the government of the Virginia land reaching north to the Great Lakes. These lands became known as the Northwest Territory. He proposed to divide the land into equal-sized states. When enough people settled in an area, it could enter the Union. These new states would have rights equal to the original thirteen. He also proposed to ban slavery in the western territories. However, this law was not passed until 1787.

When he traveled, Jefferson had problems with money. Each area had its own kind of money. The states also used money from European countries, such as Spain and Great Britain. The value of money varied from place to place. It was very confusing.

In April 1784 Jefferson wrote *Notes on the Establishment of a Money Unit and of a Coinage for the United States*. It called for a new type of money system using the decimal system. In this system everything was easily divided by ten. This is why the United States uses one hundred cents to the dollar instead of doubloons or shillings and pounds. It was passed by the Confederation Congress in 1785, after he left. Jefferson wrote in his autobiography that this was one of his chief legislative achievements.[4] Recently, many other countries have changed their currency to the decimal system.

In the fall of 1784, Congress sent Jefferson to join Benjamin Franklin in France. It was an exciting time to go overseas. Jefferson helped negotiate commercial treaties. These treaties were important. A signed treaty showed the world that the new nation existed in the community of nations.

SOURCE DOCUMENT

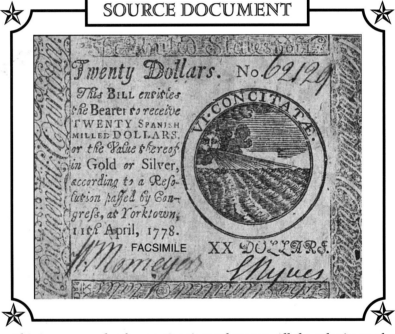

This is an example of paper Continental money. All the colonies used different forms and values of money. Thomas Jefferson persuaded the Continental Congress to establish the dollar and cents system for the United States. Unfortunately, by 1780, it had lost value. It took forty dollars to buy the same item that had cost one dollar in 1777. This created the saying, "Not worth a Continental." Alexander Hamilton's money policies stabilized the nation's money.

Benjamin Franklin retired in 1785. Jefferson became the United States minister (representative) to France. Like Franklin, he was a hardheaded diplomat. He was also respected as a scientist and a man of wide learning. Jefferson continued to work with John Adams negotiating commercial treaties. Adams was the minister to Great Britain.

Jefferson did more than diplomatic work. He also collected furniture, pictures, and china. He sent them home to Monticello. Jefferson studied the buildings around him. From then on, his designs for Monticello used French ideas. He observed events and made notes about everything. Jefferson even brought some French ideas about architecture back to America.

One of the slaves he had brought with him, James Hemings, trained under a French cook. Now Jefferson would have a superb cook at Monticello. He freed Hemings ten years later. Jefferson always made sure a slave could earn a living before he freed him or her.

He brought his daughter Martha to France with him. When little Lucy died of whooping cough, he sent for Mary. The girls stayed in a French boarding school. While there, Mary changed her name. She decided she would rather be called by the French version of her name—Maria.

Jefferson walked everywhere in Paris. While out walking on September 18, 1786, he tried to leap a fence. Unfortunately, he fell and broke his right wrist. This was his writing hand. The joint was set wrong. He ended up with a crippled hand. Eventually he was able to use the hand to write again. However, it did not work well for other things.

He had spent the last few years writing *Notes on the State of Virginia*. In it he put his thoughts about politics. He also included natural history. This included animals he knew about and some he imagined. He also wrote down his feelings about slavery. It was published in 1787. It stayed in print for many years.

He was always eager for news from America. He and his friends, James Monroe and James Madison, sent many letters back and forth. Both men had encouraged Jefferson to publish the *Notes*.

Things had changed in the United States of America. It was no longer a confederation of states. A movement to reform the Articles of Confederation led to a convention. This convention decided to create something brand new. They wrote a new constitution for the country.

Although Jefferson was not there, he influenced the convention just the same. His friends George Wythe and James Madison took part. Many of the things Jefferson had expressed in his letters over the years were included in the Constitution. One of the suggestions Jefferson had made was to divide the government into three parts. He recommended legislative, executive, and judiciary branches. In the end, the Constitution called for a Congress, a President, and a Supreme Court.

A copy of the new Constitution was sent to John

Even though he was abroad, serving as United States minister to France, Thomas Jefferson's ideas and opinions influenced the framing of the United States Constitution.

Adams in England. He sent a copy to Jefferson in France in early November 1787. In 1789, a new President was elected. The new President was Jefferson's old friend, George Washington.

The French Revolution began in July 1789. Jefferson made plans to return to America with his children. He intended to make a quick visit home in September. He would take care of debts and other business matters. Then he would return to France.

However, Washington was looking for good men to help him run the government. He asked Jefferson to stay and become the first secretary of state. Jefferson accepted.

6

SECRETARY OF STATE AND THE TWO-PARTY SYSTEM

P resident George Washington did not see any need for political parties. He gathered men who held opposite views to work under him. He chose them because they were the best men for the jobs.

Washington had several goals during his first term in office. He needed to preserve a government that represented the people of the United States. The finances of the nation needed to be put on a firm basis. This was done by raising taxes and settling debts. Relations with Great Britain and Europe needed to get back to normal.

Alexander Hamilton was his secretary of the treasury. He worked to create a strong central government. This meant the office of the President would dominate Congress. The President took control of policy making.

Jefferson disagreed with Hamilton. From his experience setting up the Virginia state government, Jefferson believed in stronger state powers and a weaker central government. When he was minister to France, Jefferson saw rich ruling classes living in luxury. He had seen poor people wearing rags and begging for food. He assumed this was caused by the strong central government there. He feared it might happen in his country.

Hamilton was in favor of an alliance with the British. He encouraged the British to invest in American industries. Jefferson favored an alliance with the French rebels in the French Revolution. He did not favor the British. Washington valued the advice of both men.

Alexander Hamilton negotiated a loan to the United States government on September 13, 1789. This loan helped stabilize the money problem. It laid a solid financial base for the government. His next step called for taxes. They would create income to pay the expenses of running a government. Hamilton also proposed that the federal government pay off the states' debts left over from the American Revolution. This would establish the federal government's credit. Plus it would convince the states to work together to pay off the joint debt.

Jefferson was against Hamilton's money policies. The Constitution did not say that the federal government *could* do these things. Therefore the Constitution limited what the federal government could do.

Hamilton argued that the Constitution did not say

he *could not* do it. Therefore it implied that the national government had broad powers. The government *could* do it.

Jefferson was against that dangerous idea. A strong government could oppress the people. These two views of the Constitution have been argued about ever since.

As secretary of state, Jefferson set up the diplomatic posts in other countries. He did not insist that his men favor the French. They were expected to try to see all sides of a question.

Hamilton and Jefferson were both members of Washington's Cabinet. The men in the Cabinet headed the Department of Foreign Affairs (now the Department of State), the Department of War, the Department of the Treasury, the National Post Office, and the Judicial Department. Each department sent daily reports to the President. Washington wrote to them asking for advice. The Cabinet members wrote their opinions in return. President Washington considered every one before he made a decision. (They did not meet together as a group until the fall of 1791.)

On July 16, 1790, Congress approved the location for the new United States capital. It was to be called the District of Columbia. Both Virginia and Maryland were supposed to donate equal amounts of land. This would make a ten-mile-square city on both sides of the Potomac River. However, only the Maryland land finally became the city.

Jefferson was active in the city planning. He helped

Washington's Cabinet during his first term included (from left to right): Henry Knox—secretary of war, Thomas Jefferson—secretary of state, Edmund Randolph—attorney general, and Alexander Hamilton—secretary of the treasury.

select architecture for the public buildings. He even submitted one of his own drawings for the capitol building under an assumed name. It was not chosen. He also organized the land sales that financed construction.

The conflict between Hamilton and Jefferson continued. President Washington usually leaned toward Hamilton's views. Hamilton's plans for industrializing the country aided strong economic growth. Creating a national bank developed industry and prosperity. So did protective tariffs on imported goods. Taxes raised money to support government expenses.

Secretary of State Jefferson continued to oppose Hamilton's actions and ideas. Hamilton even advised Washington about foreign affairs! Advice on foreign affairs was Jefferson's job, not Hamilton's. In 1793 Hamiliton urged the President to support the British against the French during a war in Europe.

Jefferson got tired of President Washington agreeing with Hamilton. He quit in 1793. It was near the end of Washington's first term. He would not try to work any more with Hamilton.

Despite Washington's wish, opposing parties did develop. These political parties centered around Jefferson and Hamilton.

Jefferson's friends were led by James Madison. They supported rule by the states and their people. They wanted a weak central government. Since they called this type of government a republic, they called themselves Republicans. These Democratic-Republicans (later called Jeffersonian Republicans) were the start of the modern Democratic party.

Hamilton's party called themselves Federalists. They supported a strong federal (central) government.

Jefferson never made speeches to gain supporters. Instead, he wrote letters to his friends from Monticello. His friends then sent these letters far and wide.

In 1796, Washington retired. He decided not to serve for more than two terms. Vice President John Adams ran for the presidency. He became the Federalist party candidate. Jefferson ran as the Republican candidate.

The two men had been friends in the Continental Congress. They had both worked on writing the Declaration of Independence. However, from this point on, they were political enemies.

It was a bitter campaign. The Republicans accused Adams of being a Royalist. They said he wanted titles and honors. They praised Jefferson for his support of the rights of the people.

The Federalists called Jefferson a coward. They published articles about his running away from the British when he was governor of Virginia. They also claimed that being a philosopher and scientist was not good training to be President.

The Constitution had not provided for two enemies campaigning against each other. John Adams won—by three electoral votes. Jefferson came in second. According to the Constitution, this made Jefferson Adams's Vice President.

Many people thought Jefferson would refuse to serve under his enemy. However, Jefferson told his advisors that he would not argue with the result. It was enough that the people had called for him. Therefore, he would serve in the office given him.

Philadelphia was still the temporary capital of the United States. Jefferson traveled there in a public stagecoach. He often traveled that way. He said it kept him in touch with the people's problems and opinions.

One of the Vice President's jobs is to be president of the Senate. Jefferson filled this office with fairness and courtesy. However, he needed guidelines. He could find nothing to help. Therefore, he wrote the *Manual of Parliamentary Practice for the Use of the United States Senate.* The Senate still uses this rule book today.

In the 1790s, France and England went to war again. The Federalists, led by President John Adams, supported England. Jefferson supported the French viewpoint. This shut him out of the government. Jefferson did not like such lack of activity.[1]

The Federalists tightened controls on their opponents. In 1798 Congress passed the Alien and Sedition Acts. These laws were used to harass people who disagreed with Federalist policies and put them in prison. Newspaper editors were especially hard hit.

The law also allowed certain government agents to open and read mail. Even letters sent to the Vice President of the United States were opened.

In response, Jefferson secretly wrote a series of

John Adams won the presidential election of 1796. Despite their strong political differences, the results of the election made Thomas Jefferson Adams's Vice President.

resolutions. They explained how the Alien and Sedition Acts were unconstitutional. He called them the Kentucky Resolutions. That way no one knew Jefferson (from Virginia) wrote them. They were a strong defense of civil liberties. They also contained a strong argument for states' rights over central government's rights.

The next presidential campaign was even more bitterly fought. This time each candidate chose a vice presidential running mate. They had no intention of having a mixed government like this last one.

Again, the Federalist congressmen decided to run John Adams for President. They chose Charles Cotesworth Pinckney of South Carolina for his Vice President. This way the two of them represented both the northern and southern states. What if Pinckney

SOURCE DOCUMENT

The Sedition Act threatened with a fine and imprisonment anyone who "shall write, print, utter or publish . . . scandalous or malicious writing or writings against the government of the United States, or either House of the Congress . . . or the President . . . with the intent to defame . . . or to bring them into contempt or disrepute; or to excite against them . . . the hatred of the good people of the United States."

The Federalists passed the Alien and Sedition Acts in 1798 to prevent those who disagreed with their policies from speaking out. This is an excerpt from the Sedition Act, which made it illegal to criticize the United States government.

received the most votes and became the President? Then surely Adams would be second. He would become Vice President.

The Democratic-Republican congressmen met in Philadelphia. At this meeting they set up the very first national platform. It described their goals. Naturally, they placed Jefferson as their presidential candidate. They offered a powerful political boss, Aaron Burr of New York, as a second choice. This slate also had a man from a southern state and a man from the North. The fourth national election of the United States was held on November 4, 1800.

Both candidates acted as if they did not care about running for President. However, it again was a bitter campaign. Federalists used the Sedition Act to arrest editors of newspapers that opposed them. Then they spread their own campaign slogans. One told voters to choose "God—and a religious President" over "Jefferson . . . and no God."[2] Federalists believed in strong laws to protect business and property. They warned that a Republican victory would lead to mob rule.

Jefferson's party concentrated on working for states' rights. They were against broad national government power. Jefferson was more concerned about the freedom of the individual.

Aaron Burr had used his political connections. He helped the Republicans win control of the New York legislature in the spring of 1800. This captured control of New York's twelve electoral votes. Now the

Democratic-Republicans had the majority of electoral votes in the presidential election.

The final vote was Jefferson—73, Burr—73, Adams—65, and Pinckney—64.[3] Jefferson and Burr had tied!

At this point, everyone expected Burr to accept the vice presidential spot. However, the highest position in the country was almost in his grasp. Burr would not step down. He forced a tie-breaking vote.

The Constitution has a law for a tie in the presidential election. The House of Representatives of Congress makes the final decision. This was the first time the rule ever had to be enforced. It was also the last.

It took thirty-six ballots, from February 11 through February 17, 1801, before Jefferson won a clear majority of votes. He won with the help of his old enemy Alexander Hamilton. The House was full of Federalists. Hamilton did not like Jefferson or his policies. However, he believed anyone would be better than Burr.[4] He convinced several representatives not to vote. This swung the election to Jefferson.

In 1796 two men of opposite political parties had won the top two spots. This time Jefferson and Burr were from the same political party. It was a contest of personalities. However, it was still an awkward situation. It looked like the Constitution needed a little tweaking to make elections run more smoothly. Jefferson would see that this was corrected during his term as President.

7

THE PEOPLE'S PRESIDENT

Jefferson called his election in 1800 a revolution. The mighty Federalists had been defeated. The Democratic-Republican party was now in charge of the government. Their man was President. They had won most of the seats in Congress as well. Their beliefs were different from the Federalists.

However, this was not like revolution in other countries. The losers were not killed. Power was transferred peacefully. Members of the other party were welcome to try to get elected again in a few years.

President John Adams made a last-minute attempt to preserve Federalist ideals. He appointed men who agreed with his ideas as judges. This filled the courts with Federalist men. These judges could throw Jefferson's laws out of the courts. Congress approved these judges by passing the Judiciary Act of 1801. These appointments were called midnight appointments. This was because they were so close to the end of Adams's term.

Jefferson was the first President to be inaugurated in the new city of Washington, D.C. It was on March 4, 1801. However, John Adams did not stay to watch it. He left town at dawn.

Jefferson refused the formality and ceremony used by Washington and Adams. He chose simplicity and dignity. He dressed in plain clothing. He did not wear a sword. He refused the gaudy, ceremonial carriage. Jefferson walked from his boardinghouse one block to the new Capitol building. Only the north wing of the Capitol had been finished. He could not, however, escape the parading artillery and rifle companies waiting for him there.

John Marshall, Chief Justice of the Supreme Court, administered the oath of office in the Senate Chamber. In his inaugural address, Jefferson stressed unity, moderation, and toleration of other people's political beliefs. "Every difference of opinion is not a difference of principle . . . We are all Republicans, we are all Federalists."[1] He emphasized the good beliefs that all Americans shared. He downplayed their differences of opinion.

To this end, one of his first acts was to ask Congress to repeal the Alien and Sedition Acts. They did. The people put in jail under those laws were released.

Unfortunately, the new President's House was not

completed in time for Jefferson's inauguration. (It was not called the White House until much later.) He was not able to move in until March 18, 1801. Jefferson described it as "a great stone house, big enough for two emperors, one pope and the grand lama."[2]

The man with no wife rattled around in this great empty house. He invited his married daughters to come live with him. He needed them to be his hostesses. They did not like to bring their children with them. They were afraid of the "bad air" of the area.

Washington, D.C., was built on a swamp. At that time no one knew that mosquitoes spread disease. People thought disease was spread by bad night air. His daughters did not stay when their hostessing duties were done.

Other times, Dolley Madison, the wife of Jefferson's secretary of state, James Madison, was his hostess. She was very active in the Washington, D.C., social scene.

Jefferson brought an informal style to the presidency. George Washington had insisted on formal dignity. Men bowed to him. Jefferson changed this. He shook men's hands, instead. All Presidents from then on shook hands.

Jefferson's red hair was now sprinkled with white. It almost looked like powder. However, he refused to powder his hair.

Jefferson avoided official receptions whenever possible. He preferred more democratic informal gatherings. Washington and Adams had continued the

Because Jefferson was a widower, Dolley Madison, the wife of Secretary of State James Madison, often acted as hostess in the President's House while Jefferson was in office.

practice of weekly formal levees. Some of these were gatherings for gentlemen. Others were for ladies. The ladies dressed in their finest clothes to honor the President and his wife. Jefferson considered this snobbery and unseemly in a democracy.[3]

He declared he would no longer hold levees. The ladies of Washington did not believe him. They arrived at the President's House on the proper day for women. However, the President was not there. He was out riding. So, the women waited. He returned, dusty and smelling of horse, to find them there.

He greeted them with the graciousness of a Virginia gentleman. "What a splendid surprise! What a delightful visit! He was overjoyed to see them! And would they not stay a bit longer?"[4]

They would not. A gentleman did not appear before ladies dirty and smelling of horse. The weekly levee was dead.

Jefferson was awkward in large groups. His voice was low and did not carry well. That is why he kept in touch with other men in government by meeting them in small groups.

One way he handled government business was at dinners. Some President's House dinners were huge formal state affairs. Others were small private gatherings. He had brought his French-trained Monticello chef, James Hemings, to Washington. Fine wines were served. Jefferson charmed politicians and diplomats with good food and clever conversation.

Jefferson put aside the rules of precedence and etiquette. Under the rules of precedence, high-ranking guests go first. He began the rule of pell-mell. This means that guests could move from one room to another in no strict order. People closest to the door entered first. Naturally, women as a group still went before the men did. Respect for women was still important. Pell-mell led to several insulted foreign diplomats. They expected the honor of going first into the dining room at Jefferson's dinners.

Jefferson dressed for comfort during the day while working on government papers. He would not dress up to greet important visitors. For example, the new British minister arrived in Washington, D.C. He dressed carefully in gold lace and his finest clothing. He expected a formal audience with the President. However, the secretary of state, James Madison, led the minister along narrow passageways to the President's study.

A shock was in store for the richly dressed minister. The President looked up from a paper-strewn desk. He rose and offered to shake hands! Jefferson was still in his shabby robe and worn-out slippers.

The British minister considered this an insult.[5] It may have been. King George had been rude to Jefferson when Jefferson was presented to the court in London in 1786. The king had turned his back and walked away.

Jefferson was a believer in the Enlightenment and the Age of Reason. As such, he did not intend to run a government based on the fears and follies of humanity.

His would be based on reason. He intended to run a government truly representative of and responsive to the needs of the people.

The nation was at peace. Jefferson slashed the money spent on the Army and Navy. He cut the budget in other ways, too. He carefully examined government spending.

Over the next few years, his good money management paid off. He stopped the tax on whiskey, which had caused the Whiskey Rebellion during Washington's term of office. Enough money still came in. He was able to reduce the national debt by one third.

Jefferson's first international conflict began with the Barbary pirates. The Barbary States of Morocco, Algiers, Tripoli, and Tunis (the North African countries) made a habit of attacking all shipping in the Mediterranean Sea. If a country paid them a bribe, called tribute, its ships were not bothered. However, if a country refused to pay, the pirates would loot its ships. They would also kidnap the sailors and passengers.

The pirates of Tripoli demanded more money. Jefferson instructed his ministers to stop paying tribute. Immediately, on June 10, 1801, Tripoli declared war against the United States. The high-ranking pasha of Tripoli cut down the flagpole in front of the United States consulate in his city. His ships began looking for United States ships to attack. For a while Jefferson ignored them.

To celebrate July 4, 1801, Jefferson reviewed the

Marines. They marched past the President's House, led by their band. It was the first presidential review of military forces.

Previous Presidents had addressed Congress in person at least once a year. Jefferson did not. He was not good at making speeches to large crowds. He sent letters to the person in charge of each legislative body. The letter sent the first year explained what he was doing. Along with the letter, he enclosed papers for the Senate and House to consider. This way they would be able to take their time replying.

By February 6, 1802, Tripoli's attacks became annoying. The United States declared war against Tripoli. Jefferson sent several warships to defend American ships in the Mediterranean. It was called the Barbary War.

Meanwhile, Jefferson signed laws creating the Army Engineer Corps on March 16, 1802. Also on that day, the first United States Military Academy was authorized at West Point. It opened on July 4, 1802.

The Judiciary Act of 1802 eliminated the positions Adams's "midnight appointments" had created. There was a fight through the courts over this act. It led to the landmark Supreme Court case, *Marbury* v. *Madison*. In February 1803 the Supreme Court declared parts of the Judiciary Act of 1802 unconstitutional. It did not abide by the rules set forth in the United States Constitution. Therefore it was to be struck from the law books.

The precedent was now established that the

Supreme Court had the final word about the law of the land. Cases concerning laws enacted by Congress and signed into law by the President may be brought before this high court. The judges decide about each case. They also make sure it agrees with the Constitution.

Meanwhile, the Northwest Territory was gradually being filled with settlers. Another state was formed from that territory. On March 1, 1803, Ohio became the seventeenth state.

Then, suddenly, the country became twice as large as before. For a mere $15 million, the territory west of the Mississippi River, called Louisiana, was purchased from Napoleon, the ruler of France, on April 30, 1803.[6] This was made official on May 2, 1803, when the Louisiana Purchase treaty was signed.

Jefferson had ordered this purchase even though it went against his beliefs. He had always believed the government should do what the Constitution said and no more. Now, however, he was faced with the fact that he had bought land to add to the country. The Constitution did not say that the President had the right to do that.

However, buying land was better than going to war over it. Congress had approved the purchase. It was done. The Louisiana Purchase became the most remembered achievement of his term in office.

Meanwhile, Captain William Bainbridge of the warship *Philadelphia* ran aground on a reef on October 31, 1803. He had been sailing after a Tripolitan cruiser.

Both his ship and crew were captured. Now the pirates had a large warship fully armed and supplied. It was important to remove this ship from their hands.

On February 3, 1804, Lieutenant Stephen Decatur defeated the Tripolitans manning this warship. He succeeded in completely destroying the *Philadelphia.* It burned to the waterline. Jefferson responded, on hearing the news, by sending every available American warship to the Mediterranean war zone.

In 1804, Jefferson's youngest daughter, Maria, died. She had married John Wayles Eppes. She died while giving birth to their second child. Former First Lady Abigail Adams wrote to console the grief-stricken father. The presidential contest and other political differences had caused these old friends to become enemies. Her letters offered friendship again between the Adamses and the Jeffersons.

Jefferson was as curious as the rest of the American citizens about the new territory of Louisiana. He appointed two men from the Charlottesville area to head an expedition to explore the territory. Captain Meriwether Lewis had been his private secretary. Lieutenant William Clark was a seasoned explorer. The two men hired other hardy explorers. They hired Native American guides. Among the Native Americans was Sacagawea, from the Snake tribe. She knew many Native American languages.

The group left St. Louis, Missouri, on May 14, 1804. Their instructions were to find a water passage to the ocean. It would be several years before they returned. The group was highly praised for their peaceful relationships with the Native American tribes they met.

People in the western areas of the country used guns to kill food and protect themselves from their enemies. In the East, guns were sometimes used for dueling in the early 1800s. Dueling was a ritual fight between two men. It had strict rules. Two angry men who wanted to fight would arrange a place and a time. They each used a special gun, which had one bullet. Their friends (called seconds) came along to make sure all the rules were followed. Honor was satisfied when the other man was wounded. However, sometimes men died.

Vice President Aaron Burr kept having conflicts with his old foe, Federalist Alexander Hamilton. Burr had not been asked by Jefferson to run for Vice President in the upcoming election. He had tried to run for New York governor and lost. Burr blamed Hamilton for this loss. Some people in the New England states tried to pull out of the United States. They wanted to set up a separate country and asked Burr to be President. Hamilton per-suaded them not to do this.

In early July 1804, Burr read an article in a newspa-per by Hamilton, condemning him. This was the last straw. Burr sent a challenge to Hamilton for a duel. They named their seconds. They were to meet in New Jersey, across the Hudson River from New York City.

Hamilton had no intention of killing Burr that day. He had plans to get the Federalists back into power.

However, he would have been called a coward by society if he backed out. He came to the dueling place early in the morning on July 11, 1804.

The honorable way to get out of a duel was to shoot in the air or simply not shoot at all. Hamilton intended to do this.

The two men stood back-to-back waiting for the order to start. They each stepped ten paces away. Then they turned to face one another. When one of the seconds gave the order, Burr fired. Hamilton did not. Burr's bullet hit Hamilton in the liver. He died painfully thirty hours later.

This is an artist's rendering of the duel between Aaron Burr and Alexander Hamilton. While Hamilton did not fire his gun, Burr shot to kill.

The electors shall meet in their respective states and vote by ballot for President and Vice-President, one of whom, at least, shall not be an inhabitant of the same state with themselves; they shall name in their ballots the persons voted for as President, and in distinct ballots the persons voted for as Vice-President, and they shall make distinct lists of all persons voted for as President, and of all persons voted for as Vice-President, and the number of votes for each, which lists they shall sign and certify, and transmit sealed to the seat of the government of the United States directed to the President of the Senate; ... The person having the greatest number of votes for President, shall be the President, if such number be a majority of the whole number of Electors appointed.... The person having the greatest number of votes as Vice-President, shall be the Vice-President, if such number be a majority of the whole number of Electors appointed....

In order to prevent the problem of having political enemies as President and Vice President, as happened in 1796, the Twelfth Amendment to the United States Constitution was approved in 1804, changing the presidential voting procedure.

When Burr realized he had killed Hamilton, he fled to South Carolina. Jefferson called him back to finish out his duties as Vice President. However, a person who murders another in a duel can never run for office again. Burr's political career had ended.

This election was easier. On September 25, 1804, the Twelfth Amendment to the Constitution had been approved. This changed the presidential voting procedure. Before, each elector could vote for two men on a list of possible Presidents. The person with the highest number of votes became President. The person with the second-highest number became Vice President. The new amendment called for one vote for a President and one separate vote for a Vice President. Both votes must, however, be for candidates within the same party.

Never again would there be a President and a Vice President of different parties (like Adams and Jefferson in 1797). Never again would two men of the same party tie for the position of President (as Jefferson and Burr did in 1801).

8

SECOND TERM AS PRESIDENT

For the presidential campaign of 1804, the Democratic-Republican party chose New York Governor George Clinton to be Jefferson's Vice President. The Federalists again put up Charles Cotesworth Pinckney of South Carolina. Rufus King from New York ran for Federalist Vice President. Pinckney was an experienced politician. However, he did not stand a chance against Jefferson's popularity. Jefferson won with 162 votes to Pinckney's 14 votes.

The first impeachment trial of a Supreme Court justice began on March 1, 1805. This was three days before Jefferson would be inaugurated for his second term. Jefferson had asked Congress to impeach a widely hated judge, Samuel Chase. Chase was the most anti-Republican member of the High Court. He insulted

82

attorneys. He attacked state constitutions, claiming that they were leaving the state wide open to Republicans and the rule of poor, uneducated people.

The House of Representatives voted to impeach Chase. By the law of the Constitution, this meant the Senate would judge the trial. Impeaching a Supreme Court justice was sensational enough. However, one more thing made it the most sensational trial of the century. Aaron Burr, Alexander Hamilton's murderer, was still president of the Senate for three more days. He would sit as chief judge.

A simple majority (over 50 percent) of the Senate found Chase guilty on a number of counts. However, they needed a two-thirds majority to impeach him. Congress could not come up with the necessary votes. Justice Samuel Chase was acquitted.

Jefferson thought the whole trial was a "farce."[1] He wanted Chase impeached. Then Jefferson could have gone on to attack the rest of the Federalist Supreme Court justices. Members of the Supreme Court are appointed for life. These men had been appointed by the previous President, a Federalist. They had been declaring Jefferson's new Republican laws unconstitutional. They did it mainly because these were not Federalist laws. Jefferson did not think the Constitution gave the Supreme Court the right to declare laws unconstitutional.

Jefferson's inauguration was a few days later, on March 4, 1805. His speech talked about the addition of

Samuel Chase, an anti-Republican and widely hated justice of the Supreme Court, became the first justice to face an impeachment trial in March 1805.

Louisiana. He said it would be better if fellow Americans settled there rather than strangers like the French or Spanish. He also talked about spending federal money on improvements like roads.

That evening a large crowd of rowdy people messed up the East Room of the President's House. This did not stop Jefferson from inviting the public to visit there. He still insisted on the rule of pell-mell.

The Barbary War drew to a close. Tripoli's main seaport was captured. Tripoli asked for peace. America signed the Treaty of Peace and Amity with Tripoli on June 4, 1805. The United States no longer paid tribute. However, the United States had to pay more ransom to free the officers and crew of the *Philadelphia.*

Unfortunately, this was not the last of the Barbary pirate problem. Pirates from other African coastal states attacked United States ships for the next ten years.

On November 15, 1805, the Lewis and Clark expedition reached the Pacific Ocean. They returned to report to Jefferson in 1806. A route via rivers to the western ocean was possible. The trip had taken them up the Missouri River. They climbed the high Rocky Mountains. Then they floated down the Columbia River to the Pacific. They had traveled eight thousand miles in over two and a half years.[2]

Jefferson had asked them to see if the land would be good for settlement. They were to treat the Native Americans they met peacefully. He also had asked for scientific records of plants and animals. Rare animals or those thought to be extinct would be best. Lewis and Clark's records were later published.

Jefferson had long been aware of fossilized bones of the woolly mammoth, which were found in western Virginia. He did not believe that a whole species of animal could become extinct. He thought that if bones were found, no matter how old, then it must exist somewhere else in the world.[3] He had asked Lewis and Clark to search for animals not known in the eastern states.

SOURCE DOCUMENT

An excerpt from the journals of Lewis and Clark dated August 12, 1805:

As they went along their hopes of soon seeing the waters of the Columbia arose almost to painful anxiety, when after four miles from the last abrupt turn of the river, they reached a small gap formed by the high mountains which recede on each side, leaving room for the Indian road. . . . They had now reached the hidden sources of that river, which had never yet been seen by civilized man; and as they quenched their thirst at the chaste and icy fountain—as they sat down by the brink of that little rivulet, which yielded its distant and modest tribute to the parent ocean, they felt themselves rewarded for all their labours and all their difficulties.

This excerpt from the journals of Lewis and Clark recounts their experiences as they neared the western coast of America.

They had found no living mammoths. They did bring other types of fossils. They also brought samples of Native American crafts. Jefferson set up a room in the President's House to display the items the explorers had collected. It was open to the public.

One of the country's new road projects led west. On March 29, 1806, Congress authorized the construction of the Cumberland Road to Ohio. Many settlers used it to reach the new Louisiana Territory.

Aaron Burr had his eye on this new half of the country. After leaving the office of Vice President, he took a vacation. He sailed down the Ohio River in a luxury flatboat. He met with Harman Blennerhasset at his island home near Parkersburg (now in West Virginia). Blennerhasset was a romantic. He conspired with Burr to "liberate" Mexico from Spain. At that time Mexico included what is now Texas. They would combine it with the Louisiana Territory to create a new country. Burr would be emperor. Blennerhasset, of course, would be a high officer.

The governor of the Louisiana Territory, General James Wilkinson, joined with Burr. The New Orleans creoles, who resented the sale of their land to the United States, also joined. Burr gathered support and money from many places.

However, General Wilkinson decided to back out. He sent a letter to Jefferson exposing the "deep dark, wicked, and widespread conspiracy" to tear apart the nation.[4] Other western settlers had also warned the President about Burr's plans.

In the fall of 1806, Jefferson issued orders to arrest Burr. He was brought to Richmond, Virginia. There he was charged with treason. The trial lasted from May 22 to October 20, 1807.

The presiding judge was John Marshall, Chief Justice of the Supreme Court. Marshall kept to the strict interpretation of the word treason. Had Burr waged war against the United States? He had not. Had he conspired with its enemies? He had not. Burr was acquitted. Planning to chop the country in half and make himself emperor was not considered treason.

The lawyers defending Aaron Burr attempted to subpoena President Jefferson to testify at the trial on June 10. Jefferson claimed they could not do this. This action was unconstitutional. The main idea of the Constitution is the independence of the legislature, executive, and judiciary. The executive (President) could not do his job if he were to be called again and again to testify in court. Therefore Jefferson refused to come. This established presidential immunity to courts.

Burr ran away to France. He stayed there until 1812. Upon his return, he took up a law practice in New York.

In 1807, Jefferson sent William Clark to the Big Bone Lick in western Kentucky. He used local workmen to collect three hundred fossil bones. They were sent to Jefferson in Washington.

Jefferson set these bones up in one of the rooms of

the President's House. He called it the "mastodon room." He opened these rooms to the general public every morning. It was the very first fossil museum in the United States. This support of scientific research gave prestige to the newly developing study of science.

Meanwhile, the two great powers in Europe, Britain and France, were at war again. By this time France, under Napoleon, had control of all of Europe. The British had control of the sea. They needed more sailors. To get them, Britain kidnapped men at home and abroad. British ship captains even boarded other countries ships, searching for escaped English seamen.

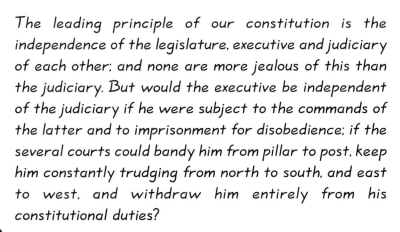

SOURCE DOCUMENT

The leading principle of our constitution is the independence of the legislature, executive and judiciary of each other; and none are more jealous of this than the judiciary. But would the executive be independent of the judiciary if he were subject to the commands of the latter and to imprisonment for disobedience; if the several courts could bandy him from pillar to post, keep him constantly trudging from north to south, and east to west, and withdraw him entirely from his constitutional duties?

President Jefferson refused to testify at the trial of Aaron Burr, claiming that the President did not have to answer the demands of the other branches of government. This is an excerpt from Jefferson's statement, in which he explains the principle of presidential immunity from the courts.

Sometimes the seamen they captured were not British citizens but Americans. Anyone with a slight British or Irish accent was captured.

In June 1807 the American warship *Chesapeake* was fired on by the British ship *Leopard.* Being unable to escape, the *Chesapeake* allowed the British to board it. The British searched and found one British deserter. Three more men were also taken. They were dragged aboard the British ship.

This happened just ten miles off the Virginia coast. The American public was furious. Jefferson could have asked for war. He would have had no trouble getting Congress to make a declaration of war.

However, he intended to use a different approach. Jefferson asked for an embargo. This meant that Americans could not buy European or British goods. It also meant that they could not send American goods anywhere in the world.

The Embargo Act against international commerce went into effect on December 22, 1807. It was intended to prevent the United States from being drawn into the war between Britain and France. However, it ended up bankrupting small American shipping lines and merchants. The larger ones already had ships at sea. They simply sent instructions for those ships not to come back to America.

The embargo caused more economic distress in America than in Europe and England. Farmers and merchants had no overseas customers for their produce. It piled up and sometimes rotted.

An interesting scientific achievement happened on August 7, 1807. Robert Fulton's steamboat *Clermont* made a trip on the Hudson River. It was not the first steamship ever built. However, it was the first commercially successful one. Within fifty years steamships would be the main type of travel on rivers. Within a hundred years steam and other engines would replace sails on oceangoing ships.

Jefferson continued his efforts to change the laws of slavery. He was still unable to get a law passed to end slavery. In 1807 a new British law ended slave trade throughout their colonies. However, the United States was no longer a colony. Its slave trade was not affected.

The British law helped Jefferson. He managed to get a law through Congress to stop importation of African slaves. The law became effective on January 1, 1808. From then on, no new slaves could be brought into the country legally. Some slaves were smuggled in, however.

The earlier complete embargo against all international shipping had not worked. It seemed to be hurting Americans more than the rest of the world. Therefore, a new act was proposed. Jefferson signed the Non-Intercourse Act on March 1, 1809. It was one of his last actions in office. This act did not forbid all trade. It simply stopped trade with Great Britain and France.

Jefferson spent eight years in office. He was highly

Thomas Jefferson refused to consider seeking a third term, in order to establish a two-term limit for Presidents.

popular as a spokesman for the common people.[5] He worked to set up an empire of liberty. The United States had grown. There were about 7 million people in the country in 1809.[6]

By the end of his term of office, Jefferson's skill in handling Congress had become apparent. Using dinners, letters, and face-to-face talk, he was able to communicate his wishes to Congress. As a result, he never had to contest the laws they enacted. He vetoed no laws.

Jefferson announced he would not accept a third term. Like George Washington, he hoped to establish a two-term limit. This would prevent future Presidents from expecting an unlimited time in office.

His secretary of state, James Madison, won the presidency in the 1808 election. In March 1809 the new President rode to his inauguration in a carriage. He offered to give Jefferson a lift. However, Jefferson said no. He and his grandson rode their own horses. They joined the crowd that followed the new President's carriage.

He wrote to a friend,

> Never did a prisoner, released from his chains, feel such relief as I shall on shaking off the shackles of power. Nature intended me for the tranquil pursuits of science . . . my supreme delight. But the . . . times . . . have forced me to take a part . . . and to commit myself . . . [to] political passions.[7]

9

RETIREMENT AT MONTICELLO

Jefferson looked forward to retirement from public office. However, his salary did not cover his expenses. He was in debt. He also had not completely paid for the things he had bought in France. Perhaps with retirement he could concentrate on managing Monticello and making a profit. Then he could pay off his debts.

He made plans for remodeling Monticello and its gardens. His oldest grandchild, Anne Cary Randolph, helped him. Several generations of Jeffersons lived at Monticello. After his daughter Maria died, her family lived upstairs. There were always children running around the place. Some were family members. Others were slave children.

The children were not allowed in his three private

rooms. These were his library, cabinet (office), and bedroom. However, when he came out from his cabinet, he would call for the children. He went horseback riding with the older ones. He organized races. He laughed at the younger children's jokes and played their children's games.

While Jefferson worked in Washington, he wrote to his grandchildren. (He had written just as often to his daughters from his workplace years ago.) He expected them to write back. Once he growled in a letter that he would send the sheriff after Ellen. She owed him more letters than he would allow.

Jefferson saved the letters he received. He made copies of the ones he wrote. His copy machine can be

This is the main house at Monticello. Jefferson designed it himself. He continually made improvements until the day he died. He so loved domes that he added them to every major building he designed.

seen at Monticello today. It uses two quill pens. He would write with one. The second pen moved with it to make a copy exactly like the first.

His cabinet was set up to be a comfortable place to study and write. He collected other labor-saving things as well. One was a swivel chair that turned. Some of Jefferson's scientific instruments are also on display there.

His bed lay in the wall between his bedroom and his cabinet. He could get up and work on something in his cabinet. Or he could roll out the other side of the bed and be in his bedroom. His clothes hung on the usual pegs in his bedroom closet. Jefferson also used a clever clothes pole with pegs. This pole had a lever to turn it around.

Throughout the house were more labor-saving things. The hall clock above the front door had two faces. One was inside the house in the hall. The other faced outside. Slaves climbed a new type of folding ladder to wind the clock.

His grandchildren loved to show off another invention to his guests. The double doors leading from the hall into the reception room were automatic doors. When a person pushed one door, both opened. This was controlled by two small drums under the floor. A figure-eight chain looped from one drum to the other. Any movement of one door moved the other.

Outdoors, Jefferson used math to design a better plow. The curve on his moldboard turned the soil over smoothly. It was better than any used in the world at that time. Plus it was made of wood. Therefore it was easy for poor farmers to make. The plow won him a gold medal from a French agricultural society.

Like most plantations Monticello was almost a self-supporting village. The food raised there supplied the workers, slaves, and family. Bricks for the house were made on the mountaintop. Carpenters framed in buildings and crafted furniture. A blacksmith worked metal and made horseshoes. Weavers made cloth. Seamstresses sewed clothing.

Every nail in the buildings at Monticello was made in Jefferson's nail factory. Extra nails were sold in near-by towns. During the agriculture depression, caused by the Embargo Act of 1807, the prices of his crops went too low to make a profit. However, money from the sale of nails helped pay expenses.

Just as the public felt free to visit George Washington, they also visited Jefferson. Hordes of visitors overloaded Monticello's ability to support them. Jefferson's steward complained, "I have often sent a wagon-load of hay up to the stable and the next morning there would not be enough to make a bird's nest. I have killed a fine beef and it would all be eaten in a day or two."[1]

The battles with the British during the War of 1812 never reached his mountaintop. The war was fought along the United States coastline. Jefferson was unable to get supplies for his nail factory, however. Plus, the lack of rain made his wheat harvest the worst ever. He was even deeper in debt than before.

Jefferson kept in constant touch with his friend and neighbor James Madison, now President of the United States. He also gave advice to his other friend and neighbor, James Monroe. Monroe was now secretary of state and acting secretary of war.

The British attacked the United States capital itself in 1814. Their forces burned several buildings, including the Library of Congress. One of the burned buildings was the President's House. President Madison was not home. He was with the troops defending the city. First Lady Dolley Madison made sure everyone got safely away from the President's House. She also rescued a full-length painting of George Washington. The picture of Washington on the dollar bill comes from this portrait.

Jefferson saw a way to lower his personal debts. His idea would also help his country. His own library was large. It was one of the finest collections of books in the country. He sold his 6,500 books to Congress for $23,950.[2] This managed to satisfy his creditors (the people he owed money to) for a time. However, he could not live without books. He began collecting more.

For years Jefferson had worked to make education available to more people. The new United States was a republic. A republic is ruled by the people's wishes. The people in a republic need to know how to read, think, and reason. They learn how to do this in schools. Once they know how, they can make better choices at election time.

In 1818 he persuaded the Virginia Legislature at Richmond to do two things. First, they paid for free elementary education for the poor. Second, they put aside money for a state university.

Jefferson proved on the map that Charlottesville was located at the very center of Virginia. It was also the center of population. Therefore the university should be built there. It is no longer the center of the state, however. The western counties of Virginia became a separate state during the Civil War in the 1860s.

Jefferson involved himself in every part of the plans. He surveyed building sites with pegs and twine and calculated the brick and lumber for each building. He hired bricklayers and carpenters. The dome on the university rotunda copies the one on Monticello. He was always ready to help if the builders had problems understanding his instructions.

Almost every day he rode his favorite horse, Eagle, down the mountain to the building site. Even when he could not get there, he watched from his little mountaintop. He could see its growth through the telescope in his cabinet.

As the opening day grew near, he drew up the course of study. He would have no religious classes. The students were free to search for knowledge in many areas. This is much like Jefferson's lifelong attitude about learning. Jefferson said it would ". . . leave everyone

This photograph of Jefferson's vegetable garden shows the marvelous view of the countryside from his mountaintop, from which he could see the ongoing construction of the University of Virginia.

free to attend whatever branches of instruction he wants."[3]

Opening day had to be delayed. Some of the professors from overseas had not arrived. The school opened in March 1825 with forty students.

Jefferson continued his interest in the school. He became a university rector. He often invited students and professors to Monticello to dine.

By the end of his life, his debts proved to be too much. His own Embargo Act had hurt his farm's economy. He could not sell his own crops. He also had loaned money to friends. Many of them did not pay back the loans.

He began plans to sell most of his property in a lottery. However, the people of America discovered his money problem. Many of them gave money to help him. This helped satisfy his creditors until his death.

In 1826, a huge Fourth of July festival was being planned for Washington, D.C. Jefferson was invited to attend. He could not come. He was ill and in great pain. In fact, he had fallen into a coma on July 2. For several days he would wake up and ask if it was the Fourth of July yet.

President Thomas Jefferson died exactly fifty years after the Declaration of Independence was signed, on July 4, 1826. President John Adams also died that day.

In their retirement, the two men had become friends again. Jefferson on his mountaintop kept in touch with the news of the day through letters. He never stopped writing to friends. He sent wise advice to President Madison and President James Monroe. He discussed his scientific studies with other interested men. Eventually people called him the "Sage of Monticello."[4]

Adams's and Jefferson's letters to each other have been saved. These letters talk about history, government, science, and philosophy.

John Adams's last words were, "Thomas Jefferson still survives!"[5] Actually, that was not true. Jefferson had died a few hours before Adams. Thomas Jefferson was eighty-three. These two men had both signed the Declaration of Independence. They had also gone on to become President. They were the only two men to have done both. They had worked together and they had been political enemies. In the end they became friends again. It was fitting that they died within hours of each other on the fiftieth anniversary of the signing of the Declaration.

Jefferson's interests covered a wide range. He studied law, diplomacy, architecture, botany, farming, raising animals, meteorology, and science. He was a husband, father, and devoted grandfather.

He never resolved his own conflicts about slavery. His house, land, and slaves had to be sold to cover his debts. Therefore, he was not able to free his slaves when he died, as George Washington did.

His will instructed that five slaves be freed. Among them were members of the Hemings family who had served him and his family so well. All of the freed slaves were skilled at a craft. They were to be given the tools of their trade to begin a new life.

In 1923 the Thomas Jefferson Memorial Foundation bought Monticello. The foundation has restored it as closely as possible to its former glory. Thousands of people visit it each year to admire his genius. The foundation also supports education programs at the University of Virginia. These follow Jefferson's ideal of scholarship.

Long before his death, Jefferson designed his own tombstone. It was to be of simple granite. This should have stopped people from stealing it for its value. He asked that his most important deeds be carved on the

This is the Jefferson Memorial in Washington, D.C. Jefferson's statue can be seen through the columns. It repeats the dome Jefferson used both for his own Monticello and for the first building of the University of Virginia.

stone. He did not count being President of the United States as one of them.

It says:

Here was Buried
THOMAS JEFFERSON
Author of the
Declaration of American Independence
of the
Statute of Virginia
for
Religious Freedom
and Father of the
University of Virginia

Over the years, the tall stone was destroyed by visitors. They chipped pieces of it to take home with them. It has been replaced. Now an even taller stone stands there.

Chronology

1743—Born on Shadwell, Virginia Colony, on April 13.

1757—His father, Peter Jefferson, dies on August 17.

1760—Enters the College of William and Mary.

1767—Begins law practice in Albemarle County, Virginia.

1768—Elected as Albemarle County representative to the Virginia House of Burgesses; signs contract to begin construction of Monticello.

1770—Shadwell burns down.

1772—Marries widow Martha Wayles Skelton on January 1; first child, Martha, born on September 27.

1774—Writes *A Summary View of the Rights of British America.*

1775—Attends Second Continental Congress in Philadelphia on June 20; writes "Declaration of the Causes and Necessity for Taking up Arms."

1776—His mother, Jane Randolph Jefferson, dies on March 31; writes the Declaration of Independence, which was accepted by the Second Continental Congress on July 4.

1776—Serves in the Virginia Assembly; writes the Virginia
–1779　Statute for Religious Freedom.

1778—His daughter, Mary (Maria), is born, August 1.

1779—Succeeds Patrick Henry as Virginia's governor on
–1781　June 1.

1782—His wife, Martha Wayles Skelton Jefferson, dies on September 6.

1783—American Revolution ends April 19; Jefferson elected delegate to Congress on June 6.

1784—Appointed by Congress to negotiate trade with European countries.

1785—Serves as minister to France.
–1789

1787—*Notes on the State of Virginia* is published; the new Constitution is ratified by the Constitutional Convention.

1789—George Washington becomes first President of the United States on April 30; Jefferson sails for home on October 22.

1790—Becomes the first United States secretary of state.
–1793

1791—Bill of Rights adopted.

1793—Resigns as secretary of state on December 31.

1794—Returns to Monticello; begins remodeling; begins to make nails to sell.

1796—Is elected John Adams's Vice President.

1797—Writes *Manual of Parliamentary Practice* for Senate.
–1800

1800—Ties for President with Aaron Burr; election decision thrown into the House of Representatives.

1801—Elected third President of the United States.

1803—Purchases the Louisiana Territory from France.

1804—Vice President Aaron Burr kills Alexander Hamilton in a duel; Twelfth Amendment to the Constitution adopted; sends Lewis and Clark to cross the Louisiana Territory.

1805—Begins second term as President.

1807—Embargo Act closes American ports to trade; Jefferson signs law forbidding import of new slaves.

1809—James Madison takes oath as President on March 4; Jefferson retires to Monticello.

1814—The British burn Washington, D.C., during the War of 1812.

1815—Sells his private library to Congress.

1817—Works on plans for the creation of the University of
–1819　Virginia.

1825—The University of Virginia opens on March 7.

1826—Dies at Monticello on July 4.

Chapter Notes

Chapter 1

1. Dumas Malone, *Jefferson and His Time, Jefferson the President—First Term, 1801-1805* (Boston: Little, Brown and Company, 1970), p. 302.

2. Daniel J. Boorstin, *The Landmark History of the American People: Volume 1—From Plymouth to Appomattox* (New York: Random House, 1987), p. 91.

3. Mary Kay Phelan, *The Story of the Louisiana Purchase* (New York: Thomas Y. Crowell, 1979), p. 136.

Chapter 2

1. Joseph Nathan Kane, *Facts about the Presidents from George Washington to Ronald Reagan* (New York: H.W. Wilson, Co., 1981), p. 38.

2. William A. DeGregorio, *The Complete Book of U.S. Presidents* (New York: Dembner Books, 1984), p. 39.

3. Saul K. Padover, *Jefferson* (New York: Penguin Books, 1952), p. 10.

4. Ibid., p. 17.

5. "Governor Fauquier to the Board of Trade, June 6, 1765," *Journal of the Virginia House of Burgesses, 1761-1765,* p. l. xvii [quoted in Willard Sterne Randall, *Thomas Jefferson, a Life* (New York: Henry Holt, 1993), p. 77.]

Chapter 3

1. Nick Beilenson, ed., *Thomas Jefferson, His Life and Words* (White Plains, N.Y.: Peter Pauper Press, Inc., 1986), p. 61.

2. Susan R. Stein, *The Worlds of Thomas Jefferson at Monticello* (New York: Harry N. Abrams, Inc., Publishers, 1993), p. 13.

3. Saul K. Padover, *Jefferson* (New York: Penguin Books, 1952), p. 23.

Chapter 4

1. Noble E. Cunningham, Jr., *In Pursuit of Reason, The Life of Thomas Jefferson* (Baton Rouge, La.: Louisiana State University Press, 1987), p. 32.

2. Cunningham, p. 36.

3. Saul K. Padover, *Jefferson* (New York: Penguin Books, 1952), p. 33.

4. Ibid., pp. 36-37.

5. *The Constitution of the United States and The Declaration of Independence* (New York: Barnes & Noble, 1956), p. 29.

6. William A. DeGregorio, *The Complete Book of U.S. Presidents* (New York: Dembner Books, 1984), pp. 43–44.

7. Cunningham, p. 50.

8. DeGregorio, p. 44.

Chapter 5

1. Noble E. Cunningham, Jr., *In Pursuit of Reason, The Life of Thomas Jefferson* (Baton Rouge, La.: Louisiana State University Press, 1987), p. 53.

2. Saul K. Padover, *Jefferson* (New York: Penguin Books, 1952), p. 45.

3. Ibid., p. 55.

4. Cunningham, p. 86.

Chapter 6

1. William A. DeGregorio, *The Complete Book of U.S. Presidents* (New York: Dembner Books, 1984), p. 45.

2. Ibid.

3. Joseph Nathan Kane, *Facts about the Presidents from George Washington to Ronald Reagan* (New York: H.W. Wilson, Co., 1981), p. 26.

4. Noble E. Cunningham, Jr., *In Pursuit of Reason, the Life of Thomas Jefferson* (Baton Rouge, La.: Louisiana State University Press, 1987), p. 233.

Chapter 7

1. William A. DeGregorio, *The Complete Book of U.S. Presidents* (New York: Dembner Books, 1984), p. 47.

2. Joseph Nathan Kane, *Facts about the Presidents from George Washington to Ronald Reagan* (New York: H.W. Wilson, Co., 1981), p. 30.

3. Saul K. Padover, *Jefferson* (New York: Penguin Books, 1952), p. 144.

4. Ibid.

5. Willard Sterne Randall, *Thomas Jefferson, a Life* (New York: Henry Holt, 1993), p. 554.

6. Ibid., p. 567.

Chapter 8

1. Saul K. Padover, *Jefferson* (New York: Penguin Books, 1952), p. 142.

2. William A. DeGregorio, *The Complete Book of U.S. Presidents* (New York: Dembner Books, 1984), p. 50.

3. Richard Sassaman, "Bone Man in the President's House, Jefferson's Passion for Science," *Cobblestone,* September 1989, p. 34.

4. Samuel Eliot Morison and Henry Steele Commager, *The Growth of the American Republic* (New York: Oxford University Press, 1962), vol. 1, p. 390.

5. "Thomas Jefferson, Third President, 1801–1809," *National Geographic,* November 1964, p. 665.

6. *World Book of America's Presidents, Portraits of the President* (Chicago: World Book, Inc., 1994), vol. 2, p. 39.

7. Nick Beilenson, ed., *Thomas Jefferson, His Life and Words* (White Plains, N.Y.: Peter Pauper Press, Inc., 1986), p. 51.

Chapter 9

1. "Thomas Jefferson, Third President, 1801–1809," *National Geographic,* November 1964, p. 668.

2. William A. DeGregorio, *The Complete Book of U.S. Presidents* (New York: Dembner Books, 1984), p. 51.

3. Ibid.

4. Dumas Malone, *Jefferson and His Time, the Sage of Monticello* (Boston: Little, Brown, 1977), vol. 6, p. xv.

5. Ibid., p. 498.

Internet Addresses for Thomas Jefferson

The home page of the people who operate Monticello, home of Thomas Jefferson

http://www.monticello.org/

Home page for the University of Virginia, founded by Thomas Jefferson

http://www.virginia.edu/

Home page for Williamsburg Online—gateway to the historical triangle of Williamsburg, Yorktown, and Jamestown

http://www.gc.net/wol/wol.html

A page about the Thomas Jefferson Memorial in Washington, D.C.

http://www.nps.gov/thje/index2.htm

A page about the Jefferson National Expansion Memorial in St. Louis, Missouri. It includes the Gateway Arch, the Museum of Westward Expansion, and St. Louis's Old Courthouse

http://www.nps.gov/jeff/generalinfo.htm

The home page of Thomas Jefferson on Politics and Government. Quotations from the writings of Thomas Jefferson

http://pages.prodigy.com/jefferson_quotes/index.htm

Further Reading

Bruns, Roger. *Thomas Jefferson*. New York: Chelsea House, 1986.

Cunningham, Noble E., Jr. *In Pursuit of Reason, The Life of Thomas Jefferson*. Baton Rouge, La.: Louisiana State University Press, 1987.

Giblin, James Cross. *Thomas Jefferson, a Picture Book Biography*. New York: Scholastic, 1994.

Hargrove, Jim. *Thomas Jefferson, Third President of the United States*. Chicago: Children's Press, 1986.

Hilton, Suzanne. *The World of Young Thomas Jefferson*. New York: Walker and Company, 1986.

Kane, Joseph Nathan. *Facts about the Presidents from George Washington to Ronald Reagan*. New York: H.W. Wilson, Co., 1981.

Lindop, Edmund. *Presidents who Dared—George Washington, Thomas Jefferson, Andrew Jackson*. New York: Twenty-first Century Books, 1995.

Meltzer, Milton. *Thomas Jefferson, The Revolutionary Aristocrat*. New York: Franklin Watts, 1991.

Padover, Saul K. *Jefferson*. New York: Penguin Books, 1952.

Phelan, Mary Kay. *The Story of the Louisiana Purchase*. New York: Thomas Y. Crowell, 1979.

Index